The fox who foxed

Story by Beverley Randell

Illustrated by Meredith Thomas

Mr. and Mrs. Fox
had five little foxes.
One day Mrs. Fox said,
"I am so hungry, but I have to
stay at home with my babies."

"I will get you a rabbit to eat,"
said Mr. Fox.

Mr. Fox said,
"I can't see any rabbits.
I'll see if I can find
a fat little hen."

He went down the hill
to the farm.

He jumped at the door
of the henhouse,
and the door flew open.

Mr. Fox ran in.

went the hens.

"A fox is in
my henhouse!"
shouted the farmer.
He ran into
the henhouse
with a stick.
He shut
the door.

The farmer hit Mr. Fox,
and Mr. Fox fell down.
"Good, I **got** him. He's dead,"
said the farmer.

Was Mr. Fox dead?
No, he was not.
He was foxing!

The farmer opened
the henhouse door.

Mr. Fox jumped up
and ran away with a hen!

"Oh, no!" shouted the farmer.
"**Stop**! Come back!"

Mr. Fox did **not** come back!
He ran home to Mrs. Fox
and the five little foxes.
"Here you are," he said.
"Here's a hen for your dinner."

"A hen!" said Mrs. Fox.
"Did the farmer see you?"

"Yes, he did," smiled Mr. Fox, "but I **foxed** him."